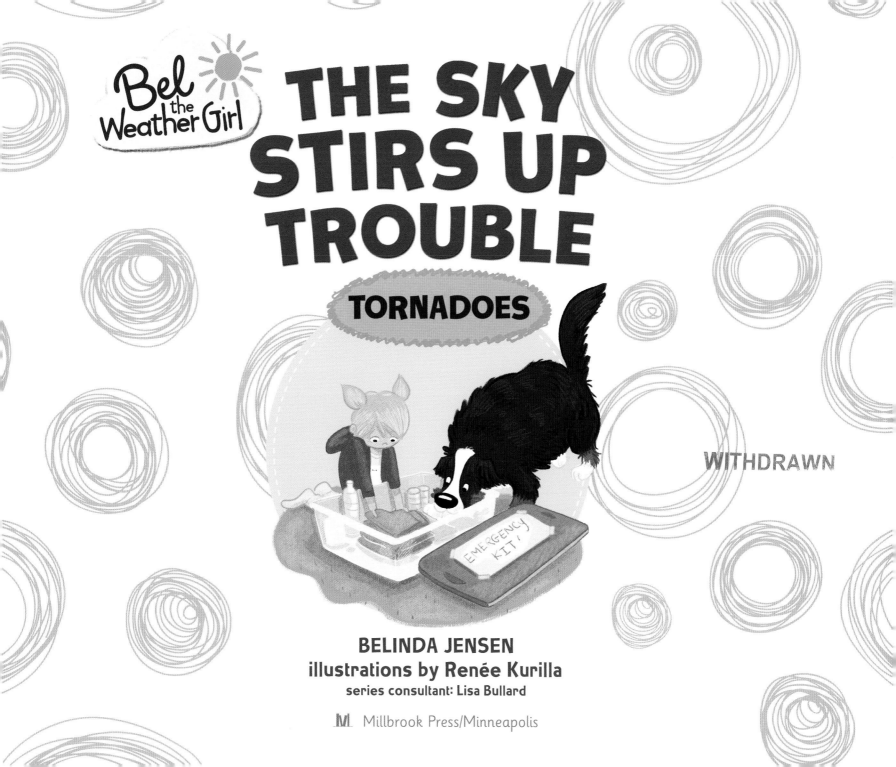

THE SKY STIRS UP TROUBLE

Bel the Weather Girl

TORNADOES

WITHDRAWN

BELINDA JENSEN
illustrations by Renée Kurilla
series consultant: Lisa Bullard

Millbrook Press/Minneapolis

To my husband David: thank you for being my partner in life and my true love.
To my Tanner: thank you for making me laugh and inspiring me with your inner
strength and passion. —B.J.

For my niece, Sydney, who is like a loveable, huggable tornado with toys! —R.K.

Millbrook Press
A division of Lerner Publishing Group, Inc.
241 First Avenue North
Minneapolis, MN 55401 USA

For reading levels and more information, look up this title at www.lernerbooks.com.

Circle background: © Natalyon/Shutterstock.com.

Main body text set in ChurchwardSamoa Regular 15/18.
Typeface provided by Chank.

Library of Congress Cataloging-in-Publication Data

Jensen, Belinda. author.
 The Sky Stirs Up Trouble: Tornadoes / by Belinda Jensen ; Renée Kurilla, illustrator.
  pages cm — (Bel the Weather Girl)
 Includes bibliographical references and index.
 Audience: 005-007.
 Audience: K to Grade 3.
 ISBN 978-1-4677-7960-9 (lb : alk. paper) – ISBN 978-1-4677-9753-5 (pb : alk. paper) –
ISBN 978-1-4677-9754-2 (eb pdf)
 1. Tornadoes—Juvenile literature. 2. Severe storms—Juvenile literature. I. Kurilla, Renée. illustrator.
II. Title.
 QC955.2.J46 2016
 551.55'3—dc23   2015015839

Manufactured in the United States of America
1 - CG - 12/31/15

TABLE OF CONTENTS

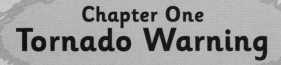

Chapter One
Tornado Warning

"Tornado siren!" called out Bel's mom. "Quick, everyone downstairs. That's the safest place in this house." Bel and her cousin Dylan hurried to the basement.

Tornadoes are high-speed, spinning winds. They form during very large thunderstorms. Most places have a siren system to sound tornado warnings.

EMERGENCY KIT!

"I'm scared!" said Dylan. "Is the house going to blow away?"

"Don't worry." Bel stood up and patted her dog Stormy. "The siren was just a warning. It doesn't mean a tornado is actually going to hit us."

After half an hour, Bel's mom said, "Good news! No tornado after all. The weather website says the warning is over. The storm has moved away. We can go back upstairs."

Go to a safe place during tornado warnings. Basements are a good choice. If you don't have a basement, go to a room with no windows or the bathroom. You can even cover yourself with pillows in the bathtub!

Bel said, "Mom, can I make a Tornado Cake with Dylan? That's how you taught me about tornadoes. Weather isn't so scary once you understand it!"

Chapter Two

The Perfect Ingredients

"A cake?" said Dylan. "I *am* hungry! Or is this a Bel the Weather Girl thing? Can we eat this cake, or does it just spin around?"

The United States has more tornadoes than any other country.

Bel's mom laughed. "Tornado Cake is real cake. I have the recipe here. I'll get out the ingredients. You two can measure them."

Bel said, "A Tornado Cake needs the perfect ingredients. Otherwise, it won't turn out right. Tornadoes are the same way."

Dylan looked outside. The sky was clearing. "Hey! Is that why we didn't have a tornado today? The storm didn't have the perfect ingredients?"

"Right!" said Bel. "A tornado needs warm air, cold air, water, and big winds."

She grabbed the sugar. "How would our cake taste if we left this out?"

"Yuck!" answered Dylan.

TORNADO INGREDIENTS:

1. Warm air
2. Cold air
3. water
4. wind

Bel laughed. "Leave out one important ingredient, and the cake doesn't work! That's true for tornadoes too."

13

Bel added sugar to the butter Dylan had put in the bowl. She handed Dylan a spoon.

"Stir them together. It takes lots of energy, right? The perfect tornado ingredients only mix during big-energy storms!"

TORNADO ALLEY

1. jet stream

2. cold dry air

3. warm dry air

4. warm moist air

Tornadoes have happened in all fifty states. Tornado Alley is an area with many tornadoes. It's in the middle of the United States. Cold northern air and warm southern air often mix there.

Chapter Three

Giant Vacuums

"Sometimes, the tornado ingredients do mix," Bel said. "Then the storm starts spinning. That makes a funnel cloud."

She pulled something out of a kitchen drawer. "This is what a funnel looks like."

"So that's a tornado?" asked Dylan.

NEWS 11

Last Month...

16

"Not exactly. Funnel clouds only turn into tornadoes if they touch the ground. Lots of funnel clouds never do," said Bel.

"It sure looks like a tornado hit in here!" Bel's mom said. "Let's clean up while the cake bakes." Bel pulled out the vacuum cleaner.

The strongest tornadoes may reach wind speeds of 300 miles (480 kilometers) per hour. They can move large objects like trucks.

"Tornadoes suck things up like giant vacuums," said Bel. "That's why we find a safe place during warnings. We want to be out of the way if the tornado ingredients mix!"

Meteorologists announce warnings when tornadoes could be nearby. Sirens sound an alert. Tornado warnings sometimes end with no tornado touchdown. But take cover every time you hear the sirens, just in case.

Chapter Four
Time for Tornado Cake!

Dylan ate his last bite of cake. "I'm glad the cake ingredients were right. And that the tornado ingredients were wrong! Let's take cake downstairs the next time there's a warning!"

"Good plan!" said Bel. "And stay tuned for tomorrow. **Because every day is another weather day!**"

Try It: Make a Tornado Cake

Ingredients

½ cup butter (1 stick) softened, plus additional to grease the pan

1½ cups all-purpose flour, plus additional to flour the pan

1 cup white sugar

2 eggs

2 teaspoons vanilla extract

1¾ teaspoon baking powder

½ cup milk

frosting of your choice

Decoration possibilities include sprinkles, mini-marshmallows, chocolate chips, coconut flakes, cold breakfast cereal, or broken pretzels.

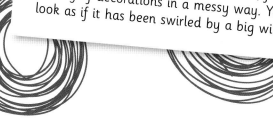

Directions

Preheat oven to 350°F (180°C). Grease and flour a 9- × 9-inch pan.

In a medium bowl, cream together the sugar and butter. Beat in the eggs, one at a time. Then stir in the vanilla. Combine flour and baking powder, add to the creamed mixture, and mix well. Stir in the milk until batter is smooth. Pour or spoon batter into the prepared pan.

Bake for 30 to 40 minutes in the preheated oven. Cake is done when a toothpick inserted in the center comes out clean.

When the cake has completely cooled, frost it. Then throw on a variety of decorations in a messy way. You want the cake top to look as if it has been swirled by a big wind!

Glossary

funnel cloud: a spinning cloud that is wide at the top and narrow at the bottom. It moves down from the bottom of a storm cloud and turns into a tornado if it hits the ground.

ingredients: different parts that combine together to make something

meteorologist: a person who is trained to study and predict the weather

tornado: high-speed, spinning winds that form during very large storms

tornado warning: a weather alert that tells people a tornado or funnel cloud has been spotted or could be forming

Further Reading

Books

Gibbons, Gail. *Tornadoes*. New York: Holiday House, 2009.
This book will teach you many more interesting facts about tornadoes.

Higgins, Nadia. *It's a Tornado!* Edina, MN: Abdo, 2010.
Read more about these huge storms.

Mezzanotte, Jim. *Tornadoes*. Pleasantville, NY: Weekly Readers, 2010.
See photographs and learn more about tornadoes in this book.

Websites

Tornadoes
http://www.nws.noaa.gov/om/brochures/owlie/Owlie-tornadoes.pdf
Learn more about tornadoes while coloring these fact-filled pages featuring Owlie from the National Weather Service.

Tornadoes
http://www.ready.gov/kids/know-the-facts/tornado
At this site, you can play a game that will help you learn how to build an emergency kit for your home.

Tornado Model
http://pbskids.org/dragonflytv/show/tornados.html
Watch this video from PBS Kids Go! to see two students build a tornado model so they can learn more about these big storms.

Index

LERNER
e
SOURCE

Expand learning beyond the printed book. Download free, complementary educational resources for this book from our website, www.lerneresource.com.